Cover: HMS 'Amphion', 1944 (see Plate 20)

Note: All the items illustrated in this booklet are part of the Science Museum collections

A Science Museum
illustrated booklet

BRITISH WARSHIPS

1845-1945

by B. W. Bathe

Her Majesty's Stationery
Office London 1970

Introduction

In the relatively short period of one hundred years, from 1845 to 1945, remarkable changes and advances took place in the design, propulsion and armament of the fighting ship. In this booklet it is only possible to give a very brief outline of these changes and of the evolution of some of the warships which served in the Royal Navy during the period, while the choice of illustrations has been dictated by the rather limited scope of the collection of models of steam warships at the Science Museum.

The first half of the 19th century saw the final development of the sailing warship in the British Navy. From about 1820 steam power was used for small naval vessels, but as paddle-wheels and engines were considered very vulnerable to gun-fire, the steam vessels were first employed as fleet auxiliaries and not as fighting ships with the battle fleet. However, the size of naval paddle steamers was gradually increased and in 1840 steam warships took part for the first time in an offensive action of any magnitude. The 1st Class frigate HMS *Terrible* (Plate 1), launched in 1845, had a displacement of 3289 tons and when first commissioned was one of the most powerful steam war-vessels in the world.

Trials arranged by the Admiralty during the 1840's showed the superiority of the screw propeller over the paddle-wheel for ordinary sea purposes. For naval purposes the screw propeller, in addition to its greater mechanical efficiency, possessed the great advantage that it worked below the surface of the water and further that the engines also could be below the water-line leaving no vital parts exposed to gunfire. From 1847 onwards the use of the propeller was extended to the large ships of the Navy, the practice being to fit existing sailing ships-of-the-line with engines and a propeller for use in addition to the sails. The propellers were so arranged that they could be raised out of the water when the ships were under sail and at the same time the funnels could be lowered. The first line-of-battle ship to be specially designed for screw propulsion was HMS *Agamemnon*, of 80 guns, launched in 1852.

The introduction of explosive shells which could be fired with accuracy and safety greatly increased the destructive power of gunfire and it became necessary to provide additional protection for the vulnerable parts of a wooden warship. New and existing wooden vessels were therefore provided with an armour of iron plates. The first iron-built sea-going armoured warship HMS *Warrior* (Plate 4) was launched in 1860 and after 1863 only small British naval vessels were built of wood. Initially the design of the iron-built warships was influenced by that of the old wooden ships and the main armament was arranged, in broadside, along the length of the vessel, which was still fitted with heavy rigging and a large spread of sail in addition to the engine.

The continued increase in the size and power of guns brought about the next development in battleship design and the production of the central-battery ship. The larger guns could not be mounted in the old extended broadside manner and from about 1865 the heavy armament was arranged behind thick armour in a citadel situated amidships. In the 1870's sail power for propulsion was abandoned. while the need for maximum protection and maximum arc of fire led to the introduction of the revolving armoured turret for the guns. The barbette mounting came into use in 1877 and was generally adopted for the larger warships. The gun was carried on a revolving platform with the base containing the turning machinery and ammunition hoists protected by a stationary ring of very heavy armour.

Advances in warship design and construction during the last decades of the 19th century and the early years of the 20th century included such new features as the use of steel for the hull and armour, and the introduction of the armoured protective deck and solid bulkheads. In consequence of these changes, as well as improvements in the guns and their mounting and in engines and boilers the size, speed and fighting power of successive classes of battleships were greatly increased.

Although the twin screw battleships HMS *Lord Nelson* (Plate 10) and her sister ship HMS *Agamemnon* were of 16,500 tons displacement and showed notable advances in armour and gunpower, these vessels and all previous battleships were rendered obsolete by the construction of HMS *Dreadnought* of 17,900 tons displacement. Built in great secrecy and completed in a year from the time the keel was laid down, the *Dreadnought*, first commissioned in September 1906, was faster and carried two and a half times as many 12-in. guns as any existing warship. This super battleship's greatly increased speed was obtained by the use of steam turbines, then for the first time fitted in a large war vessel, to drive quadruple propellers. Originally built as an experiment, the *Dreadnought* proved so successful that future battleship designs of all naval powers followed similar lines. HMS *Monarch* (Plate 13), launched in 1911, was a battleship of the 'Improved Dreadnought' class. This group of warships was the first to have all the main armament in turrets on the centre line and further progress, including 15-in. guns and oil-fired boilers, was made with the battleships of the *Queen Elizabeth* class launched in 1913-1915. HMS *Nelson* and *Rodney* the only British battleships completed in the years between the two world wars carried a main armament of nine 16-in. guns in three triple mountings and a secondary armament of twelve 6-in. guns in twin mountings. These two vessels, launched in 1925, were built in accordance with the conditions of the Washington Treaty of 1922 and their standard displacement was 1,000 tons less than the pre-scribed limit of 35,000 tons. Five battleships of the *King George V* class, with a main armament of ten 14-in. guns in two quadruple turrets and one twin turret, were all completed in the period 1941-1942 and the development of the British battleship came to an end in 1946 with the completion of HMS *Vanguard* (Plates 18 and 19). This battleship, the last to be built for the British navy and the largest warship ever built in Great Britain, was broken up in 1960.

As early as 1912 seaplanes had been launched from temporary flying-off platforms erected on British warships. During the 1914-18 war merchant ships and warships were converted into aircraft carriers but HMS *Hermes* launched in 1919 was the first ship to be specially designed by the Admiralty as an aircraft carrier. HMS *Illustrious*, completed in 1941, was the first aircraft carrier to be fitted with an armoured flight deck.

For some fifteen years after the introduction of iron-clad warships the cruising work of the Royal Navy was carried out by unarmoured steam frigates and corvettes. The first 'protected' cruiser was launched in 1875: HMS *Magicienne* (Plate 8), launched in 1888 and fitted with a protective steel deck, was a typical example of the small cruiser of the period, while HMS *Diadem* (Plate 9) and the vessels of the same class built in 1896-98 were large 'protected' cruisers without side armour. Battle cruisers carrying an armament almost equivalent to that of a battleship, but with lighter armour and capable of high speeds, came into service in 1908 with the *Invincible* class of 17,410 tons displacement, and culminated in HMS *Hood* of 42,100 tons launched in 1918.

The progressive development of the small cruiser, required for scouting and screening duties, also continued and HMS *Glasgow* (Plate 12) represents the type of lightly armoured cruiser being built for the Royal Navy just before the war of 1914-18. By the end of the war a cruiser of similar dimensions carried an armament of six 6-in. guns, three 4-in. anti-aircraft guns and twelve torpedo tubes in triple mountings. Post war construction included thirteen 10,000 ton cruisers armed with 8-in. guns and capable of a speed of 32 knots. As originally designed these cruisers were protected by an armoured deck but additional side armour at the waterline was fitted when the vessels were reconstructed during 1935-1938. The various classes of cruisers, all fitted with side armour, completed for the British navy between 1939 and 1945 included cruisers of 10,000 and 8,000 tons displacement carrying 6-in. guns in triple mountings.

The development of an accurate self-propelled torpedo made it necessary to provide the fleet with small fast vessels suitable for launching these torpedoes against enemy ships. HMS *Lightning* (Plate 7) built in 1877 and afterwards known as 'Torpedo Boat No. 1', was the first torpedo boat in the British Navy.

The term 'torpedo boat destroyer'—soon shortened to 'destroyer'— was first applied to a larger type of torpedo boat designed in 1892 and HMS *Tartar* (Plate 11) launched in 1907 was one of the first ocean-going destroyers in the British Navy to be driven by steam turbines and oil-fired boilers. There was an increase in the size, speed and armament of destroyers during the 1914-18 war and flotilla leaders of 1,530 tons displacement, carrying five 4.7-in. guns and with six torpedo tubes in triple mountings came into service. Developments between the wars included a further general increase in dimensions with increased accommodation, considerably higher speeds and an extended radius of action. Torpedo tubes in quadruple mountings were first fitted in HMS *Antelope* (Plate 17) and the other A class ocean-going destroyers, all launched in 1929. Nineteen new classes of destroyers came into service between 1940 and 1945, the largest vessels being the 'Battle' class fleet destroyers of 2,315 tons launched in 1943-45.

The first submarine built for the British Navy was launched in

October 1901 and was one of a class of five 'Holland' type boats used for experimental and training purposes. The American 'Holland' submarine, propelled by internal combustion engines when on the surface and by electric motors when submerged, was the archetype of the practical submarine torpedo boat. Over the next ten years the design of British submarines included the introduction of external water ballast tanks and the use of heavy oil engines in place of petrol motors for surface propulsion. Watertight transverse bulkheads first fitted to the 'E' class submarine (Plate 15) of 1912-17 provided increased hull strength thus allowing deeper dives to be made with safety and by the end of the 1914-18 war the submarine was established as a major war weapon.

1   HMS 'Terrible' 1845

Small paddle steamers were used by the British Navy during the 1820's as tugs and dispatch vessels. From about 1830 larger naval steamers were built and by the end of the decade steam paddle frigates formed part of the fighting strength of the Navy.

The 20-gun paddle frigate *Terrible* built at Deptford in 1845 with a length of 226 ft and a displacement of 3189 tons, was at that time one of the most powerful steam war-vessels in the world. The wooden hull of the frigate was specially constructed to resist the stresses of her heavy armament and machinery; the frames being fitted so closely together that they formed an almost complete body before the external planking was added.

The *Terrible* was propelled at a speed of 10.9 knots by paddle-wheels 34 ft in diameter, driven by a pair of 'Siamese' engines of 400 nominal hp, with four cylinders each 72 in. diameter by 8 ft stroke. The original armament consisted of eight 68 pdrs and eight 56 pdrs together with three 12 pdrs and a field gun.

During the Crimean War the *Terrible* took part in operations around Sebastopol, and by her excellent steaming qualities was enabled to weather the disastrous gale in the Black Sea in 1854. In 1869 the frigate assisted in towing the first Bermuda floating dock across the Atlantic. She was broken up in 1877.

The aquatint from a painting by W. Knell, reproduced on the opposite page, was published in 1846.

2   HMS 'Highflyer' 1851

In order to test the relative efficiencies of the screw propeller and the paddle-wheel, a series of trials took place in 1843-45 between HMS *Rattler*, the first screw vessel constructed by the Admiralty, and HM Paddle frigate *Alecto*. The most spectacular of the trials was one in which the two vessels were tied stern to stern and made to steam full speed ahead ; the *Rattler* then towed the *Alecto* stern foremost at a speed of 2.8 knots. As a result of these trials the screw propeller was shown to be much more suitable than the paddle-wheel for warships and was then adopted for ships of the British Navy.

HMS *Highflyer* a ship-rigged, wooden, corvette launched at Blackwall in 1851, was a typical example of a small warship fitted with a propeller which could be raised out of the water when the ship was under sail. Her engines, of 770 indicated hp, were of the horizontal direct-acting type and during trials a speed of 9.8 knots was obtained. The corvette was 192 ft long, with a displacement of 1775 tons, and was armed with twenty 8-in. guns and one 10-in. pivot gun, all carried on the upper deck.

The *Highflyer* took part in actions in the Black Sea during the Crimean War and later served in the East Indies and Far East. She was broken up in 1872.

3 HMS 'Racoon' 1857

The *Racoon* was a ship-rigged corvette, built of wood to the designs of Sir Baldwin Walker, and launched at Chatham in 1857. She was a sister ship to HMS *Challenger*, which was built in 1858, and was employed in 1872-76 on the famous scientific expedition which bears her name.

These corvettes and another of the same class, the *Clio*, also built in 1858 were 200 ft long with a breadth of 40.5 ft and a displacement of 2160 tons. The armament of the *Racoon* consisted of two 68-pdr guns on traversing mountings on the upper deck and twenty 8-in. guns on the main deck. The engines, of the horizontal direct-acting type with two cylinders 64 in. diameter by 3 ft stroke, indicated 1486 hp and gave a speed of 11 knots. There were four tubular boilers and bunker accommodation for 250 tons of coal.

The *Racoon*, after service in the Mediterranean and off the coasts of North and South America, was broken up in 1877.

4   HMS 'Warrior' 1860

The success in action of armoured floating batteries in 1855, led to the development by the French Government of an armoured type of sea-going wooden-built frigate. The British Admiralty followed with the construction of HMS *Warrior*, the first iron-built and armoured warship ; and thus opened a new era in the history of the fighting ship.

Built at Blackwall by the Thames Ironworks and Shipbuilding Co. from designs prepared by Sir Isaac Watts in conjunction with John Scott Russell, the *Warrior*, launched in 1860, was 380 ft long with a displacement of 9210 tons. Her side armour, consisting of belts of iron plates 4.5 in. thick backed by 18 in. of teak planking, made the warship practically proof against the most powerful guns then in use.

The armament of the *Warrior* was changed from time to time, but in 1867 it consisted of four 8-in. guns and twenty-eight 7-in. guns. The propelling engines were of the horizontal trunk type with cylinders 104.6 in. diameter by 4 ft stroke. On trials in 1861 a speed of 14.35 knots was realised, the engines making 54 revs per min. and indicating 5470 hp.

After many years of useful service with the fleet the *Warrior* was used as a training ship and floating workshop. Since 1929 the vessel has been used as an oil pipe-line pier at Pembroke.

5 HMS 'Eclipse' 1867

The construction of large warships in wood for the British Navy was discontinued soon after the advent of sea-going iron-built armoured vessels, but timber was used until about 1870 for many of the small corvettes and sloops.

The 6-gun sloop *Eclipse*, built of wood and launched at Sheerness in 1867, was 212 ft long with a displacement of 1698 tons. The vessel was armed with two 7-in. muzzle-loading, rifled guns, mounted amidships on traversing slides for firing on either side, and two 64-pdr guns were carried on each broadside with alternative ports for bow and stern fire. The direct-acting trunk engines developed 2100 indicated hp and gave a speed of 13 knots. The propeller could not be raised, but under sail alone a speed of 11 knots was achieved.

Like many of the corvettes and sloops of the period, the *Eclipse* spent much of her time on distant stations. After serving long commissions in North and South American waters, she was refitted and rearmed and in 1880 sent to the East Indies. In 1884 the *Eclipse* was laid up in reserve and in 1888 converted into a store hulk for mines.

6   HMS 'Arrow' 1871

In the 18th and 19th centuries small shallow-draft vessels were specially designed to carry one or two large guns. They were intended for work in coastal waters or river estuaries, where larger warships could not operate, and were used principally to attack the enemy's shore-batteries or to supplement their own shore-batteries in defensive actions.

The gunboat *Arrow*, built of iron at Greenwich in 1871, was only 85 ft long, with a draft of 6.4 ft, but was armed with a 10-in. muzzle-loading gun weighing 18 tons. The gun was mounted on a platform, which could be lowered by gearing so as to increase the stability of the vessel when at sea. The *Arrow* was propelled by twin-screws driven by two sets of reciprocating engines giving a speed of 8.5 knots.

Nineteen other coast-defence gunboats of the same class were built in 1870-73. Most of these vessels had long service ; the *Arrow* was not broken up until 1922.

7 HMS 'Lightning' 1876

The invention of the self-propelled underwater torpedo, and in particular the improved accuracy which was obtained with this weapon in 1876, made it necessary to provide small fast vessels suitable for launching these torpedoes against enemy ships.

HMS *Lightning*, later re-named 'Torpedo Boat No. 1', was built by John I. Thornycroft & Co. Ltd. at their Chiswick works in 1876. The galvanised steel hull was 84.5 ft long and was well subdivided by transverse watertight bulkheads. The propelling machinery consisted of a two-stage compound engine which could develop 478 indicated hp and on trials a speed of 19.4 knots was attained, which was reduced to 18.5 knots when the torpedoes were on board. The armament comprised of two 14-in. diameter Whitehead torpedoes, stowed amidships on transporting carriages and rails, which were discharged by means of compressed air from a pivoted tube mounted in the bows.

'Torpedo Boat No. 1' was sold in 1910.

From 1881 onwards, steel completely replaced iron in the construction of the hulls of British warships and the protective iron deck, introduced in 1875, was developed into an arched steel deck, which by its form reduced to a minimum the flooding which would result if the ship's side was pierced near the water-line, while the curved or inclined surfaces deflected projectiles.

The protective deck was also used in vessels of the cruiser class, and the *Magicienne*, a cruiser launched in 1888, was provided with an arched steel deck 1.5 in. thick on the flat and 2 in. on the slopes, starting from 5 ft below the water-line and rising 1 ft above it amidships.

The *Magicienne*, built by the Fairfield Company at Glasgow, was 265 ft long with a displacement of 2950 tons and was one of the last warships to be fitted with horizontal engines ; these were of the three-stage expansion type, developing 9280 indicated hp and giving a speed of 18 knots. The coal bunker capacity was 400 tons, which gave a radius of action, at 10 knots, of 6000 miles. The armament included six 6-in. breech-loading guns—the breech-loading gun had been finally adopted for the British Navy in 1880—and four torpedo tubes.

The principal duties of the *Magicienne* and her sister ships the *Marathon* and *Melpomene* were police work and 'showing the flag' on the coasts of Africa and America. The three cruisers were sold in 1905.

9 HMS 'Diadem' 1896

The eight ships of the *Diadem* class, built in 1896-1902, were the last heavy cruisers to have hulls without side armour and protected only by a curved armoured deck. The cruisers were 462 ft long overall with a displacement of 11000 tons, and carried a main armament of sixteen 6-in. guns. Two set of four cylinder, vertical inverted triple-expansion engines were fitted, with thirty water-tube boilers of the Belleville type. An improved pattern of boiler was fitted to the last four ships of the class and the designed horse-power increased from 16500 to 18000.

The *Diadem* built by the Fairfield Company at Glasgow and launched in 1896, realised a speed of 20.65 knots with 17188 indicated hp during full-power steam trials in 1898. During the 1914-18 war she was converted into a minelayer and was sold in 1921.

Although a further advance was made in the armour and armament of the battleship *Lord Nelson* and her sister ship the *Agamemnon*, the dimensions and general structural arrangements were very similar to those of the typical British battleship of the previous ten years. The vessels were 443.5 ft long overall, with a displacement of 16500 tons, and the armour included a complete belt of Krupp steel on the water-line, 12 in. thick amidships tapering to 6 in. forward and 4 in. aft. An armament of four 12-in. guns and ten 9.2-in. guns provided a powerful concentration of gun power, but this was the last time a mixed main armament was fitted in a British warship.

These were also the last British battleships to have twin screws and reciprocating engines. This machinery consisted of two sets of vertical triple expansion engines. During full-power trials in 1908 the *Lord Nelson* made a speed of 18.7 knots with 17445 indicated hp.

The *Lord Nelson* was built by the Palmers Shipbuilding and Iron Co. at Jarrow-on-Tyne and launched in 1907. After serving as Flagship of the Channel Fleet in 1914, she took part in the operations at the Dardanelles in 1915-16 and was sold in 1920.

The larger model shown in the plate opposite represents the *Tartar*, one of the first ocean-going destroyers in the British Navy to be driven by steam turbines and oil-fired boilers. Built by Thornycroft & Co. at Southampton in 1907, the *Tartar* was 272 ft long overall with a displacement of 860 tons, and carried an armament of three 12-pdr guns and two torpedo tubes. The Parsons steam turbines drove triple screws and on trials a speed of 35.67 knots was achieved.

The *Tartar* served with the Dover Patrol during the First World War and was sold in 1921.

The smaller model shown in the plate, represents Torpedo Boat 'No. 17' built in 1907 at Dumbarton by W. Denny & Bros. Armed with two 12-pdr guns and three torpedo tubes, the torpedo boat was 180 ft long and propelled by triple screws driven by Parsons turbine machinery. The boilers were oil-fired and the designed speed of 26 knots was exceeded on trials. During 1905-9 thirty-six vessels of this type, intended for coastal or defensive service, were built for the British Navy.

A new type of cruiser, intended for scouting duties and capable of a speed of 25 knots, was introduced into the British Navy in 1904. These vessels, of less than 3000 tons displacement and very lightly armed, were soon succeeded by classes of larger and more heavily armed 'light' cruisers with much better sea-keeping qualities.

The *Glasgow* and four other cruisers of the same class, all launched in 1909, were of 4800 tons displacement and 453 ft long overall. They were armed with two 6-in. guns, ten 4-in. guns and two torpedo tubes. Protection to the vital parts was afforded by an arched protective deck of nickel steel, extending from end to end in the vicinity of the water-line and with the sloping sides continued well below that level. The propelling machinery was of the Parsons turbine type, with four lines of shafting driving four screws.

The *Glasgow*, built by the Fairfield Shipbuilding and Engineering Co., Ltd., at Glasgow and completed in January 1911, achieved a speed of 26.7 knots on trials. The cruiser was present at the Battle of Coronal in November, 1914 and at the Battle of the Falklands in the following month. She also took part in the destruction of the German cruiser *Dresden* in 1915. The *Glasgow* was sold in 1926.

13   HMS 'Monarch' 1911

The *Monarch* and her sister vessels *Orion*, *Conqueror* and *Thunderer*, all completed in 1912, were battleships of the 'Improved Dreadnought' type. This was the first group of British warships to have an armament of ten 13.5-in. guns and also the first to carry the whole of the main armament in turrets on the centre line. The 13.5-in. guns were mounted in pairs in five hooded barbettes, with the second and fourth barbettes raised sufficiently above the deck level to allow their guns to fire over the bow and stern guns respectively. This provision, coupled with the centre-line disposition of the guns, gave a direct fire of four guns both forward and aft while permitting the use of all ten guns on either broadside. For use against torpedo craft there was a secondary armament of sixteen 4-in. guns.

The four battleships, each 581 ft long overall with a displacement of 22500 tons, were propelled by quadruple screws driven by Parsons turbine engines and on trial they all exceeded the designed speed of 21 knots. External protection included a water-line belt of armour 12 in. thick and booms with steel nets were used as a defence against torpedoes.

The *Monarch*, built by Armstrong, Whitworth & Co. at Elswick was launched in 1911 and in 1916 served with the 2nd Battle Squadron at the Battle of Jutland. In 1925, she was used as a fleet target and sunk by gunfire.

During the First World War a number of heavily armed, shallow draught vessels were built or acquired for the British Navy. Known as monitors, they were intended principally for long range bombardment of the coast of Belgium.

HMS *Humber* was one of three monitors which were under construction, by Vickers Ltd at Barrow-in-Furness for the Brazilian Navy, but were, at the outbreak of war, taken over by the British Admiralty.

The vessel was built of steel, with the hull divided into a larger number of water-tight compartments by means of both transverse and longitudinal bulkheads. Protection was provided by belts of 2-in. armour at each side of the vessel.

With a length of 265 ft and a displacement of 1260 tons, the *Humber* was propelled by twin screws, driven by two sets of triple expansion engines, developing 1450 indicated hp and giving a speed of 12 knots. The main armament consisted of two 6-in. guns mounted in an armoured turret on the forward part of the upper deck and two 4.7-in. guns aft.

After taking part in the bombardments of German forces established on the Belgian coast, the *Humber* served in operations in the Dardanelles and the Gulf of Aqaba. In 1920 she was sold to a Dutch company and converted into a floating crane.

15 HM Submarine 'E' Class

More than fifty 'E' class submarines were built for the British Navy between 1912 and 1917. Twenty-seven of the class were lost during the First World War when many of these vessels rendered splendid service and performed the most arduous duties.

The 'E' class submarines were 181 ft long with a submerged displacement of about 800 tons and were fitted with external ballast tanks. They were the first British submarines with internal subdivision by water-tight bulkheads and the first with beam torpedo tubes. The armament varied, with from three to five torpedo tubes, and one 3-in. or one 12-pdr gun.

Two sets of Diesel engines were fitted for surface propulsion, with electric motors driven from accumulators for under-water work. The surface speed was 15 knots and when submerged 10 knots was attained. When on the surface the accumulators could be recharged by means of the Diesel engines, with the motors acting as generators.

16 HMS 'Tobago' 1918

The development of destroyers during the First World War was marked by an increase in dimensions, due to the necessity for remaining at sea over extended periods. The increased freeboard had obviated the need for a raised turtle-deck over the fore-peak, which had been a prominent feature of earlier destroyers (see Plate 11).

The *Tobago* was one of the five ocean-going destroyers known as the Thornycroft 'S' class, and built at Southampton in 1918-1919 for the British Navy. These destroyers were 275.75 ft long overall with a displacement of 1087 tons and carried an armament consisting of four 21-in. torpedo tubes in pairs on two turntables and two 18-in. torpedo tubes on athwartship racks under the bridge. In addition, there were three 4-in. guns and one 2-pdr pom-pom. The vessels had two propellers driven by geared steam turbines and on trials the *Tobago* attained a speed of 38.21 knots.

The *Tobago*, launched in July, 1918, struck a mine in the Black Sea in November, 1920.

The construction of destroyers for the British Navy was discontinued for five years after the end of the First World War, but two experimental destroyers were built in 1924-26 and the destroyers of the first post-war class were launched in 1929. This group of very successful ocean-going vessels, known as the 'A' class, included the *Antelope*, built at Newcastle, by R. & W. Hawthorn Leslie & Co, Ltd and completed in 1930.

The 'A' class destroyers were 323 ft long with a displacement of 1330 tons. The armament consisted of four 4.7-in. guns, two 2-pdr pom-poms and eight 21-in. torpedo tubes arranged in groups of four on turntables. The two-shaft arrangement of Parsons single-reduction geared turbines was designed to give a speed of 34 knots. This speed, however, was exceeded in each vessel of the class, the *Antelope* reaching 36.8 knots on trials.

During the Second World War, the *Antelope* served in the Atlantic and the Mediterranean, taking part in the operations against the *Bismarck* in 1941 and with the Malta Convoys in 1942. She was broken up in 1946.

18   HMS 'Vanguard' 1944

The *Vanguard*, the largest warship ever built in Great Britain and the last battleship to serve in the British Navy, was built at Clydebank by John Brown & Co, Ltd, being launched in 1944 and completed in 1946. Designed by Sir Stanley Goodall, with an overall length of 814.3 ft and a standard displacement of 44500 tons, the vessel was protected by armour 16 in. thick in parts, distributed so as to provide the maximum defence against gun-fire and air attack, while the water-tight subdivision of the hull was so thorough that access to various compartments could only be obtained by vertical shafts. The engine-rooms and boiler-rooms were arranged in four self-contained units with a special system of humidity control which maintained an even temperature in the Arctic or in the tropics. The Parsons single-reduction turbines were supplied with steam by eight Admiralty three-drum water-tube boilers and developed 130000 total shaft hp, giving a sea speed of 29.5 knots.

19   HMS 'Vanguard' amidships

The *Vanguard* was armed with eight 15-in. guns, sixteen 5.25-in. guns and sixty 40-mm anti-aircraft guns; with four 3-pdr guns for saluting purposes. The 15-in. guns were mounted originally in the battle-cruisers *Courageous* and *Glorious*, but were removed in 1924 and added to the reserve of weapons, when these ships were converted into aircraft carriers.

The *Vanguard* was used for the Royal Tour to South Africa in 1947, for which purpose the Admiral's quarters in the after superstructure were altered into Royal apartments.

The battleship was refitted at Devonport in 1947-48, served in the Mediterranean in 1949, and as flagship of the Home Fleet in 1952-54. She was again refitted in 1954-55, placed in reserve in 1956 and broken up in 1960.

The sixteen 'A' class submarines, completed between 1945 and 1948 were intended for service in the Far East, which called for increased surface speed and endurance. Special attention was given to habitability, since environmental conditions in the Far East would be much more severe than in home waters or the Mediterranean.

The *Amphion*, the first of the class, was laid down as the *Anchorite* in 1943, but was re-named and completed in 1945. The hull was fabricated in sections by automatic welding. Each section had the plates running fore-and-aft and the circumferential joints had to be manually welded later. The vessel was propelled by twin screws, with 8-cylinder Diesel engines and electric motors. The maximum speed on the surface was 19 knots and when submerged 8 knots. Snort air valves, equivalent to the German 'Schnorkel' apparatus, were fitted and enabled the Diesel engines to be run with the submarine submerged at periscope depth. The armament included one 4-in. gun, one 20 mm anti-aircraft gun and ten 21-in. torpedo tubes.

The *Amphion*, built by Vickers-Armstrongs Ltd. at Barrow-in-Furness, was 281.7 ft long, with a surface displacement of 1385 tons and a submerged displacement of 1620 tons. The 'A' class submarines were later reconstructed and streamlined with a high enclosed fin conning tower.

Science Museum illustrated booklets

Published by
Her Majesty's Stationery Office
and obtainable from the
Government Bookshops listed
on cover page iv (post orders
to PO Box 569 London SE1)

7s each (by post 7s 4d)

Printed in England for
Her Majesty's Stationery Office
by W. Heffer & Sons Ltd.
Cambridge

Dd. 147311 K100